Teamwork!

By Mary Lindeen

Scott Foresman
is an imprint of

Glenview, Illinois • Boston, Massachusetts • Chandler, Arizona •
Upper Saddle River, New Jersey

Photographs

Every effort has been made to secure permission and provide appropriate credit for photographic material. The publisher deeply regrets any omission and pledges to correct errors called to its attention in subsequent editions.

Unless otherwise acknowledged, all photographs are the property of Pearson Education, Inc.

Photo locators denoted as follows: Top (T), Center (C), Bottom (B), Left (L), Right (R), Background (Bkgd)

ISBN 13: 978-0-328-46907-9
ISBN 10:   0-328-46907-6

This boy and his dog are a team. They work together. The boy throws the toy. The dog jumps up and catches it.

This man and his dog are a team too. He is training the dog. Someday it will be a guide dog.

Guide dogs are "eyes" for blind people. This dog sees danger that the man cannot. It might see stairs or a hole in the sidewalk. The dog will guide the man around the danger.

Hearing dogs are "ears" for deaf people. Deaf people cannot hear. This dog listens for noises such as a ringing telephone or a baby crying. It lets its owner know what's happening.

This dog helps its owner at home. The dog can open doors. It can pick up things on the floor. It can even answer the phone!

Some monkeys can help too. This monkey does things its owner cannot do. Its small hands can even put a CD into a CD player!

Have you ever heard of a helping pig? Pigs are very smart and very strong. They learn quickly. This pig will be a helping animal someday.

This cat is a helping animal too. She visits people in a nursing home. They like to hold her and pet her. She makes them happy.

Guide horses are miniature horses. They are trained to do the same things guide dogs do.

Helping animals are hard workers. They keep their owners safe. They may even save their owners' lives. In return, the owners take care of their animals. That's teamwork!